W9-DGE-419

IRAN

Land of the Peacock Throne

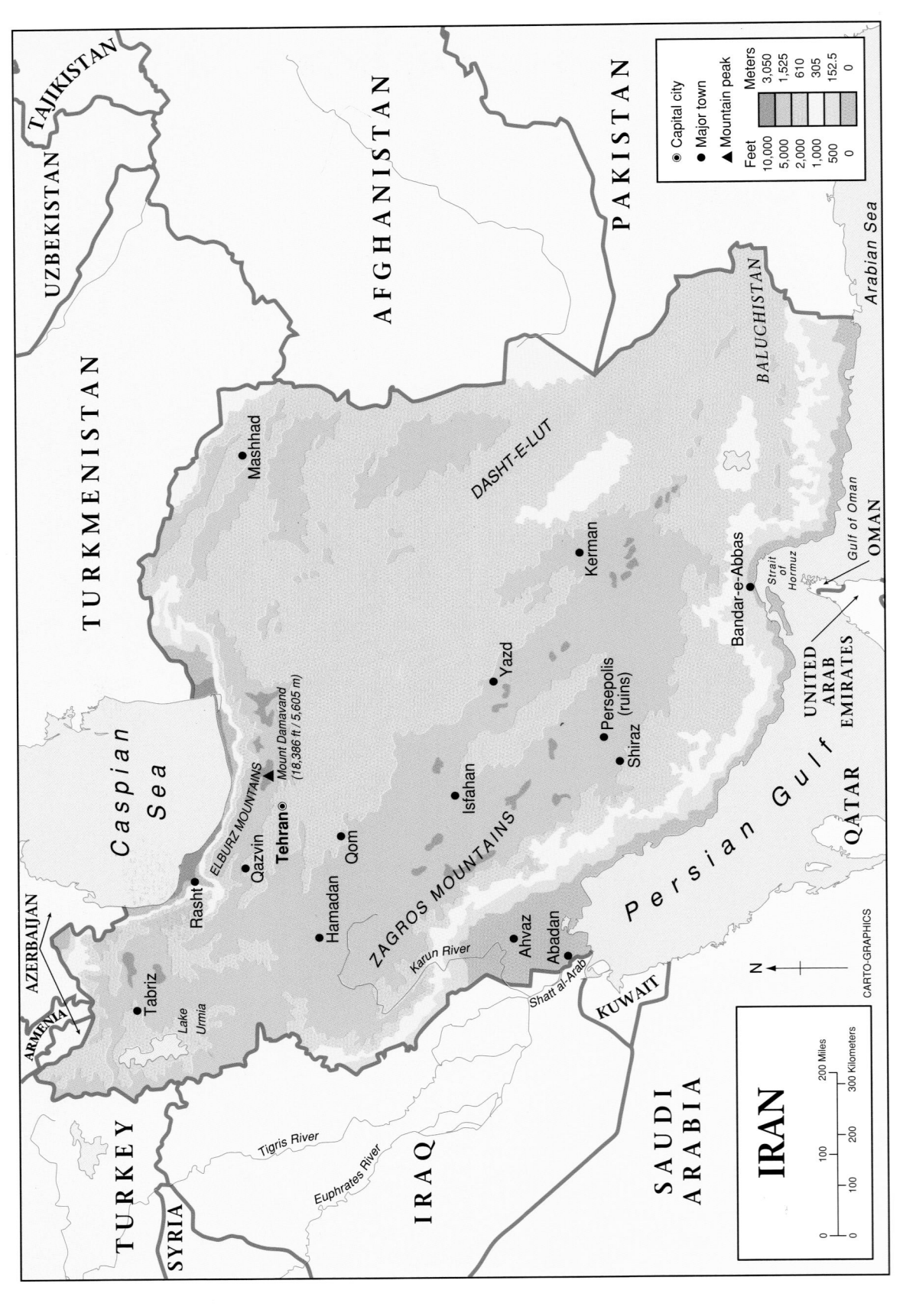

TAJIKISTAN

UZBEKISTAN

TURKMENISTAN

AFGHANISTAN

PAKISTAN

Arabian Sea

BALUCHISTAN

Capital city
Major town
Mountain peak

Feet	Meters
10,000	3,050
5,000	1,525
2,000	610
1,000	305
500	152.5
0	0

Mashhad

DASHT-E-LUT

Kerman

Bandar-e-Abbas

Strait of Hormuz

Gulf of Oman

OMAN

UNITED ARAB EMIRATES

Caspian Sea

Yazd

Persepolis (ruins)
Shiraz

Mount Damavand
(18,386 ft / 5,605 m)

ELBURZ MOUNTAINS

Tehran

Qazvin

Qom

Isfahan

QATAR

Rasht

Hamadan

ZAGROS MOUNTAINS

Persian Gulf

Tabriz

Lake Urmia

Karun River

Ahvaz
Abadan

AZERBAIJAN

ARMENIA

N

KUWAIT

CARTO-GRAPHICS

Shatt al-Arab

SAUDI ARABIA

TURKEY

SYRIA

IRAQ

Tigris River

Euphrates River

IRAN

200 Miles
300 Kilometers
100	200
100	200
0	0

EXPLORING CULTURES OF THE WORLD

IRAN

Land of the Peacock Throne

William Spencer

BENCHMARK BOOKS

MARSHALL CAVENDISH
NEW YORK

With thanks to Helen Rafiy, educator and Middle East specialist, for her reading of the manuscript.

Benchmark Books
Marshall Cavendish Corporation
99 White Plains Road
Tarrytown, New York 10591-9001

© Marshall Cavendish Corporation 1997

All rights reserved. No part of this book may be reproduced or utilized in any form or by any means electronic or mechanical including photocopying, recording, or by any information storage and retrieval system, without permission from the copyright holders.

Library of Congress Cataloging-in-Publication Data

Spencer, William
    Iran: land of the peacock throne / by William Spencer.
        p.   cm. — (Exploring cultures of the world)
    Includes bibliographical references (p.).
    Summary: An introduction to the history, geography, culture, and people of Iran.
    ISBN 0-7614-0336-1 (lib. binding)
    1. Iran—Juvenile literature.   [1. Iran.]   I. Title. II. Series.
DS254.5.S67   1997
955—dc20   96-22455
                                                          CIP
                                                           AC

CODMAN SQUARE

MAR 1997

Printed in Hong Kong
Book design by Carol Matsuyama

Front cover: An Iranian boy in traditional dress
Back cover: A mosque in Isfahan

Photo Credits

Front cover and page 39: ©Shandiz/Courtesy of the Mission of Islamic Republic of Iran; title page and pages 44, 45: Courtesy of the Mission of Islamic Republic of Iran; back cover and page 40: ©Johan Elbers/International Stock Photo; page 6: ©Werner Forman/Art Resource, NY; page 10: Bruce Dale/©National Geographic Society; pages 11, 26, 31, 38, 42, 47: ©Eslami Rad/Gamma Liaison; page 13: ©Duclos-Gaillarde/Gamma Liaison; page 15: ©George Holton/Photo Researchers, Inc.; page 16: ©Fred Maroon/Photo Researchers, Inc.; page 19: ©Francis Lochon/Gamma Liaison; pages 20, 32, 34, 48: ©Chip Hires/Gamma Liaison; page 23: ©Bill Wrenn/International Stock Photo; page 25: ©D. Driscoll/Gamma Liaison; page 27: ©Pascal Maitre/Gamma Liaison; page 28: ©Paolo Koch/Photo Researchers, Inc.; page 50: ©Stock Boston/Owen Franken/PNI; page 52: ©Emil Muench/Photo Researchers, Inc.; pages 54, 57: ©Beatriz Schiller/International Stock Photo; page 55: ©Alexis Duclos/Gamma Liaison

J
DS254.5
.S67
1997

CD

Contents

The history and the culture of Iran were captured by artists in the form of Persian miniatures—small, detailed paintings. Here, a miniature from the A.D. 1500s shows people preparing a meal.

1
GEOGRAPHY AND HISTORY

The Power and
the Majesty

The Mighty Rustam

Once long ago, in the land we call Iran, lived a great warrior named Rustam. He was famous far and wide for his mighty deeds of strength and skill. He was so tall that his head reached the clouds. With one finger, he could throw a brick for many miles. He could outwrestle an elephant or a lion. Rustam rode a magic horse named Raksh.

One day, Rustam's friend the King was captured by the Divs. These demons held him prisoner. A message reached Rustam, begging him to rescue his friend.

Rustam had performed many great deeds, but he had never tangled with the dreadful Divs. The valiant warrior did not hesitate, however. He mounted Raksh and rode off toward the distant land of the demons, where he had never been before.

On the first night out, Rustam slept in a forest. A lion crept up on him and was about to leap, when Raksh—who never slept—killed the beast with one powerful kick.

For days Rustam and his faithful horse rode across a vast desert. They could not find water anywhere. Rustam was almost dead of thirst when, by a miracle, a spring of pure, cold water bubbled up at his feet.

Refreshed, Rustam rode on. Finally, he entered the land of the Divs. No ordinary human could harm these creatures, who could change shape in the blink of an eye. As Rustam rode along, a Div in the form of a huge fire-breathing dragon charged at him. Rustam defeated the monster with one blow of his double-bladed battle-ax.

Other Divs attacked Rustam as he rode through their territory. Some took the forms of wild animals; others became trees with thorny branches. Rustam fought them all off, with the help of his magic steed. But his greatest test remained: to rescue his friend.

The prison in which the King was held was guarded by the Great White Div, the most feared of all the demons. As Rustam neared the prison, the Great White Div suddenly appeared before him as a monster breathing fire from a pair of huge jaws and roaring in a terrifying voice. Rustam swung his great ax, and the monster fell. Immediately, it changed form and became a giant boulder. But Rustam would not be stopped. He picked up the boulder and smashed it against a mountainside. Again, the Div changed form—this time into a cloud. Rustam reached high into the sky and shredded the cloud with his bare hands. In this way, he forever broke the power of the Divs and rescued his friend the King.

Legends such as the story of Rustam help make Iranians proud of their history and the deeds of their past. In books, Rustam is called a *Pahlavan,* or "mighty warrior."

Ring of Mountains

Iran sits high above sea level on a great stretch of flat land called a plateau. The average height of the plateau is 3,300 feet (1,000 meters). This vast country—it is about three times the size of Texas—is partly encircled by mountain ranges. The mountains have always provided the country with natural protection from invaders.

The two main ranges are the Zagros and the Elburz. The Zagros Mountains run along the western side of the plateau. The Elburz lie in the north, between the Caspian Sea and Tehran, the capital city. Iran's highest peak, Mount Damavand, is located in the Elburz. It rises 18,386 feet (5,605 meters). Covered with snow year-round, Mount Damavand has long been considered a holy place.

Country at a Crossroads

Iran's location makes it an important crossroads of the world. It shares its borders with seven other countries: Iraq and Turkey to the west; Armenia and Azerbaijan to the northwest; Turkmenistan to the north; Afghanistan and Pakistan to the east. The Caspian Sea lies to the north. The Persian Gulf and the Gulf of Oman lie to the south.

An important waterway runs between Iran and Iraq, a powerful neighbor to the west. It is called the Shatt al-Arab (shot al-ah-ROB). It is formed by the coming together of the Tigris and Euphrates Rivers before they flow into the Persian Gulf. The Shatt al-Arab stretches 127 miles (203 kilometers). It is deep enough for oceangoing ships, such as oil tankers, to travel through. It is very important for trade. Iran and Iraq have had disputes over ownership of the Shatt al-Arab for hundreds of years. It is one of the reasons why the two countries fought a bitter war during the 1980s.

A Dry Land

In the mountains, summers are mild, but winters are bitterly cold. Snow and freezing temperatures are common. Most of Iran, however, has a climate similar to that of the American Southwest. It has long, hot, dry summers and mild winters.

Herders and nomads travel through the dry desert regions of Iran, such as this area near the city of Shiraz.

Much of Iran's land is desert—*dasht* (dahsht), in Farsi, the major language of Iran. Except in the region along the Caspian Sea, very little rain falls. The east-central area, called the Dasht-e-Lut, has one of the harshest climates on earth. There, during the long summer months, the "Wind of 120 Days" blows. It brings with it dust and very hot temperatures. It seems as if it will never end.

Iran has few lakes and rivers. Only one large river in the country, the Karun, has water all year long. Many others dry up completely in the hot summer and disappear into the desert, leaving behind large salt flats.

Rich in Resources

The low rainfall and huge expanses of desert make farming difficult in Iran. But Iranian farmers have managed to make the land bloom through the use of irrigation. They grow a great variety of crops. The most important ones are rice, wheat, sugarcane, sugar beets, barley, and tea. The country is

10

also famous for its pistachios. Iran is one of the world's largest producers of these tasty green nuts. Oranges, grapefruits, and Persian limes are grown along the coast of the Caspian Sea. Sweet Persian melons also come from this region.

Sheep and goats are also important to Iran's economy. There are about 54 million of these animals in Iran! Most of them are owned by nomads—people who move from place to place, seeking fresh grazing lands for their animals. They use the animals' meat and milk as sources of food. The wool is used in weaving beautiful Persian carpets. Many of these carpets are sold outside Iran.

Iran has many other valuable resources. The one that makes the most money for the country is petroleum. Oil was first discovered there in 1908. This industry was largely run by foreign oil companies until the 1950s, when the Iranian government took greater control of oil production and sales—and a greater portion of the income from oil sales.

Thanks to irrigation, farmers are able to grow abundant crops in some regions of Iran.

Iran also has large deposits of natural gas, iron ore, and coal. It is one of the world's largest producers of sulphur, which has many uses. It is used to make chemicals, fireworks, and dyes. Several years ago, geologists discovered a large amount of phosphate rock, which is used in fertilizers.

A Long History

The name *Iran* (ee-RAN) is short for *Aryanem*, "Land of the Aryans." Wandering Aryan tribes from central Asia moved south and settled in the area nearly 4,000 years ago. The land had been occupied by other peoples, though, for several thousand years before the Aryans arrived.

There were two main Aryan tribes: the Medes and the Persians. In the mid-500s B.C., Cyrus, a Persian chief, overcame the Medes and made himself master of most of their land. Cyrus and the rulers who followed him conquered many lands outside Iran. They established the world's first empire. Cyrus also started the first Persian dynasty—a line of kings or emperors from the same family who rule for many years.

The Persian emperors founded a number of important cities. One was Persepolis. It had splendid buildings, great palaces, temples, and royal tombs. Only their ruins can be found today.

The Persian emperors set up the first postal service in the world. Mail carriers rode swift horses or racing camels. They traveled on roads paved with brick. These roads also allowed the emperors' soldiers to move quickly from place to place to keep control of the people.

The great Persian Empire controlled a large part of the world. But it was hard for the rulers to manage so many different peoples. The emperors often made the mistake of

The columns of Persepolis are all that remain of this once spectacular ancient city.

going to war with distant peoples to gain land. One such people, the Greeks, defeated several Persian armies. Around 330 B.C., a young Greek king named Alexander conquered the entire Persian Empire in just a few short battles! For this reason, he is known as Alexander the Great. His dream was to conquer the world, but when he died in 323 B.C., his vast empire fell apart.

A few years later, the Parthians, a Persian tribe, won control of the empire's Iranian provinces. They were very skilled in warfare. They were superb horsemen and archers. It was said that a Parthian archer could shoot a quiver full of arrows into an enemy while riding away at full speed!

The Coming of the Arabs

The Parthians were followed by the Sassanians, another line of kings. But in the A.D. 600s, a new enemy challenged their rule. An army of men from the deserts of the Arabian Peninsula, to the southwest, swept into Iran. They were the Arabs, a nomadic people. These warriors rode racing camels and fast horses. They shouted *Allah o akbar!* ("God is great!").

The Arabs crushed the Persian army and killed the last Persian king. It was only the second time that the Persian people had been brought under foreign control. The first time had been by Alexander the Great.

The Arab conquest was different from Alexander's, however. The Arabs did not just want to control new territory. They were inspired by a new religion, Islam (ISS-lam), which was started by the Prophet Muhammad. The Arabs' main goal was to convert the people of Iran to their religious beliefs.

Islam is an Arabic word meaning "submission" or "surrender." The Arabic name for God is Allah (ah-LAH). One who "surrenders" or "submits" to Allah is called a Muslim (MUHZ-lim).

The Arab conquest changed the lives of the Iranian people in many ways. Not only did most Iranians become Muslims, but they also started using another language: Arabic. Before long, many Arabic words replaced Farsi (Persian) ones.

The world of Islam became the center of a great civilization, and Iran was an important part of it. Muslim scholars made many contributions to such fields as medicine, map making, astronomy, and physics. A golden age of learning and culture lasted for many years.

Then, in 1258, the Arab civilization in Iran came crashing down. The Mongols—a central Asian people—invaded

Iran in search of new pastures for their sheep and goats. They conquered and destroyed many cities. After a while, the Mongols settled in Iran and were converted to Islam.

Iran's Peacock Throne

While the Mongols were in power, various Turkish tribes wandered into Iran. They became Muslims, and they competed with the Mongols and other groups for power.

The chief of one Turkish group decided to make a deal with the religious leaders of Islam, the mullahs (MOO-lahs). He promised to protect the mullahs and not interfere with their religious authority over the people. In return, they would support his claim to become the shah, or ruler, of Iran. He established a new line of shahs—called the Safavids.

The greatest Safavid ruler was Shah Abbas I, who became ruler in 1588. Under his rule, the Persian Empire grew

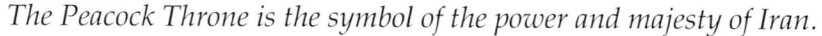

The Peacock Throne is the symbol of the power and majesty of Iran.

Delicate arches make up this bridge in Isfahan.

and grew, until it stretched from the Tigris River in the west to the Indus River in the east. But it was Abbas's quest for beauty that we can most easily see today. He chose the old city of Isfahan, in the center of present-day Iran, as his capital, and he made it a work of art. He built many mosques (mahsks)—Muslim houses of worship—which were decorated with green, gold, and turquoise tiles. He constructed magnificent palaces and planted gardens with pools framed by cypress and sycamore trees. He built graceful, arched bridges over the little river that runs through the city. The city is so famous for its beauty that Iranians have a saying: "To see Isfahan is to see half the world."

In the 1700s, a general led the Iranian army in a successful invasion of India. The army brought back many valuable things. The greatest prize was the Peacock Throne. It was covered with peacock feathers—the symbol of royalty. It glittered with 26,000 precious jewels woven into the fabric. From then on, the shahs of Iran were crowned while sitting on it. The throne became the symbol of the power and majesty of Iran.

The Modern World

About 150 years ago, the world outside Iran began to change rapidly. The inventions and processes of the Industrial Revolution brought about a need for raw materials.

Because of its location and resources, Iran found itself a focus of European countries' competition for these materials. A shah from that time thought that he could help his country benefit from this competition. But the shah signed agreements that gave away control over Iran's resources to foreigners. The country, despite its wealth of resources, was very poor.

The Pahlavi Dynasty

In 1925, a new leader, Reza, was crowned shah of Iran. He took the ancient name Pahlavi for the new dynasty he hoped to start.

Reza Shah, as he was known, wanted to make Iran a modern country like those in Europe. He made some progress in the short time that he ruled, from 1925 to 1941. During World War II, which started in 1939, Reza Shah supported Germany. As a result, the armies of Great Britain and the Soviet Union occupied Iran in 1941. Reza Shah was forced to leave the country. He turned over the Peacock Throne to his twenty-two-year-old son, Muhammad Reza Pahlavi.

The Islamic Revolution

By 1978, Muhammad Reza Pahlavi had ruled Iran for thirty-seven years. He wanted to follow his father's dream for Iran, so he concentrated on improving the economy.

Most Iranians, however, remained very poor, though the shah and his family were very rich. The people were not allowed to criticize the shah publicly—if they did, they might

THE IRANIAN GOVERNMENT

The Islamic Republic is governed under a Constitution approved in 1979. It was written to agree with the laws of Islam. It sets up a government of three independent branches, with a president, the *Majlis* (House of Representatives), and a court system.

Iranians over age fifteen have the right to vote. The president is elected for a four-year term. Elections to the *Majlis* are also held every four years. There are no political parties, so candidates run as independents, or as members of a trade or profession, or as religious leaders. Iran has a Supreme Court and lower courts. Final authority rests with the highest-ranking ayatollah, known as the "supreme legal guide."

be arrested or even killed. In secret, though, many Iranians complained about his wealthy lifestyle. The mullahs said that the shah was not a good Muslim. The shah did not obey the laws of Islam, they said, and he allowed women too much freedom. Women were even appearing in public without chadors (CHAH-doorz)—veils and body coverings. What is more, the mullahs said, television, movies, and rock music were having a bad effect on Iran's young people.

The leader of the mullahs was the Ayatollah Ruhollah Khomeini (ko-MAY-nee). For years Khomeini worked to overthrow the shah. In 1979, he succeeded. The shah realized that he was opposed by almost all his people, and he left the country, never to return. The Ayatollah Khomeini now took control. He called his new government an Islamic republic.

The Islamic Republic

A "republic" is a form of government in which the people rule through elected representatives. Iran's president is elected, and a House of Representatives, called the *Majlis* (MAJ-lee), makes the laws. But the true rulers of the nation are its religious leaders. All laws must be approved by the highest-ranking members of the mullahs—called ayatollahs. Before the laws go into effect, they must be judged to be in agreement with the laws of Islam.

The Ayatollah Khomeini ruled Iran with an iron hand from 1979 until his death in 1989. Under his rule, the people were forced to follow many of the old strict laws of Islam. Women had to wear the chador whenever they were in public. Also, people were not allowed to practice any other religion but Islam. Khomeini's police arrested and killed the supporters of the shah. Many thousands of people died.

The Ayatollah Khomeini inspired great loyalty and passion in his followers— and great anger in his critics.

Iran also lost the friendship of other countries. It became known for terrorism—using violence to bring about some political change. In 1979 and 1980, Iranian students occupied the United States Embassy in Tehran and held 52 Americans hostage for more than a year. In the 1980s, Iran fought a bitter and bloody war with Iraq. Several million people were killed on both sides.

Today religious leaders still rule Iran. Since Khomeini's death in 1989, the government has concentrated on improving the economy. It has also worked to strengthen its relationships with other countries.

*Almost all Iranians are Muslims. Women in Iran wear either the traditional
chador or a long, raincoatlike garment.*

2
THE PEOPLE

Who Are the Iranians?

Iran's nearly 65 million people have much in common with one another today. But there are also many differences that identify Iranians as belonging to different ethnic groups.

These various peoples have different backgrounds. Their ancestors settled in Iran from other areas over time. Today, they might differ in how they look and speak, in the ways that they make a living, in how they dress, and in the kinds of homes they live in.

Often their ways of life have been shaped over many generations by Iran's geography. For instance, people living along the low-lying Caspian Sea came to eat foods and build homes that were very different from those of people in the drier mountainous areas.

A World in Common

Despite such differences, most people in Iran have several important things that bind them together. First, of course, the different groups in Iran have lived there for many centuries.

Thus, Iranian people share a long cultural heritage and sense of belonging.

The major language in Iran is Farsi, once called Persian. It is spoken by 58 percent of the population and is the language of government and business. After the Arab conquest of Iran in the A.D. 600s, Farsi was written in Arabic letters, and the language picked up many Arabic words. Some ethnic groups have their own languages, such as Azeri Turkish and Kurdish. But Farsi remains a unifying bond. Many Iranians also speak English and French.

Perhaps the strongest unifying force in the country, though, is the Islamic religion. Islam is a major part of the daily lives of most Iranians. It plays an important role in the government and culture of Iran as well.

Land of Islam

Almost all Iranians today—98 percent—are Muslims. Their common religious beliefs help to unite the many groups in this huge nation.

The vast majority of the Muslims in Iran belong to the branch of Islam called Shia (SHE-uh). Sometimes this branch is called Shiite (SHE-ite). Ninety-five percent of Iranians are Shia Muslims. The other Muslims belong to the branch of Islam called Sunni (SOON-nee). This balance between Shias and Sunnis in Iran is unusual. In most other Muslim countries, there are far more Sunnis than Shias.

The religious differences between Shia and Sunni beliefs have to do mainly with tracing the leadership of Islam from the Prophet Muhammad. These differences have caused much anger and conflict between Shias and Sunnis since the early days of Islam.

Nearly all the Muslims in Iran belong to the Shia branch of Islam.

The Persians

The biggest ethnic group in Iran is the Persians, sometimes called ethnic Iranians. They form about one half of the people of the country today. Their ancestors came to Iran from central Asia nearly 4,000 years ago.

Over the years, the Persians came to control the country. Their customs, language, and system of government gradually became dominant. Today Persians live throughout the country rather than in one particular region. They can be found in both the country and in the city. They make their living in a great variety of ways; they are farmers, business people, government workers, and teachers, for example.

23

The Azeri Turks

The next-largest ethnic group is the Azeri Turks. They live in northwestern Iran. They are descended from Turkish tribes that invaded Iran a thousand years ago.

The Azeris speak a form of Turkish as well as Farsi. Many of them would like to have more independence from the national Iranian government.

The Kurds

Another important ethnic group is the Kurds. They are Sunni Muslims (as opposed to the majority of Iranians, who are Shias). The Kurds live mostly in the Zagros Mountains, along the borders with Iraq and Turkey, in small villages of close-knit families. They raise sheep and goats and grow their food in small plots of land in the valleys of the mountains. Their language is similar to both Farsi and Turkish.

The Arabs

The Arabs, another large ethnic group, live mostly in the area along Iran's border with Iraq. Their ancestors moved to that region after the conquest of Iran by Arab armies. It is a hot, desertlike area. Its only vegetation is the camel thorn shrub. Only camels can eat its leaves.

Non-Muslims

While most of the people of Iran are Muslims, not all are. Iran, for example, has a small population of Jewish people. The country is also home to a small group of Armenians. They have their own language and form one of the world's oldest Christian communities. Many of Iran's carpet dealers are Armenians.

Another small non-Muslim group is the Zoroastrians (sore-oh-AS-tree-uhnz). At one time, the Zoroastrian religion was the official religion of ancient Persia. The Zoroastrians consider fire to be sacred. Fire is the symbol of good in the world, while darkness is the symbol of evil.

The Bahais (bah-HIZE) are another religious group. The Bahai religion grew out of Islam from the visions of a Muslim holy man in the mid-1800s. Baha Ullah (bah-ha OO-lah) taught that men and women are equal and that all religions are related. His teachings aroused the anger of the mullahs in Iran, who said that he was trying to destroy Islam. He was forced to leave the country. Today, the Bahais in Iran are treated as enemies of Islam. Many have had to leave the country since the Islamic Revolution of 1979.

A small Jewish community still practices its traditions in Iran.

City Life

In recent years, Iran's population has become more urbanized. About 43 percent of the people live in the countryside, but 57 percent reside in towns and cities. City and town dwellers generally lead busy lives, hurrying to work and school. The way these people live—how they earn a living, socialize, and keep a home—is similar to the way city dwellers live elsewhere in the world.

As in many modern cities, traffic jams can be a problem in Iran's large urban centers.

There are actually two kinds of cities in Iran. One is modern, with tall buildings, wide streets, traffic lights, and long lines of cars. The other kind of city is ancient and in some ways seems like a large village. The two kinds of cities often exist side by side.

The area around Tehran, Iran's beautiful capital city, is a good example of this. Tehran has tall buildings of glass and steel, fine homes with lawns and gardens, and parks with bubbling fountains. Its streets are wide. (But with 6 million people and many cars, there are still huge traffic jams!) Next to modern Tehran is a city hundreds of years old. It used to be completely surrounded by a high wall to protect it from enemies. The heart of this old city was, and still is, the bazaar, or market. Another important center of life in the old city is the mosque.

Men sit and read in an open plaza in the heart of Tehran.

Country Life

In small country villages, people's lives are tied to their daily chores and to the rhythm of the seasons. There is always a lot of hard work to do at home and in the fields. Women take care of their families and homes. These houses are usually made of mud brick, which help to keep them cool. The women carry water from the village's well, and they bake their bread at home. Fathers and sons go out early to their fields or to a neighbor's field if they have no land of their own. They work there from sunrise to sunset. Younger sons, and often daughters, go out with their shepherd's crooks, taller than they are, to guard the family's flocks of sheep and goats. These days, many children also attend school.

Since most of Iran is so dry, farming families must work very hard to make their living from the soil. Most farmers depend on irrigation to grow their crops. They draw water

27

Donkeys are used for many different kinds of jobs in Iran. Here, a boy uses a donkey to carry oil.

from underground wells. Then the water is moved through channels into the fields. Many Iranian farmers have pumps that bring the water up to these irrigation channels. But not all farmers can afford the pumps they need.

Some farmers, however, are within reach of a unique irrigation system that was developed centuries ago in Iran. Underground tunnels called *qanats* (KAH-nats) were built to bring water down from mountain springs and across the plateau. Some of the *qanats* are more than a thousand years old, and many are hundreds of miles long!

Iran's farmers often keep mules and donkeys, which some use for plowing the soil. Dromedaries—camels with one hump—were once very common. They were used to haul water from wells and to carry goods long distances. In the past, long trains of camels could often be seen, roped together with a single rider on the lead animal. The goods they carried might be taken all the way to China. Today, such products are carried long distances by modern modes of transportation, including trucks and freight trains.

28

The Nomadic Peoples

Iran has a number of nomadic tribes. Nomads are people who have a wandering lifestyle, rather than a settled one, like farmers and city people do. In the past, Iran's nomads were independent under their tribal chiefs, called sheikhs (SHAKES). Today, their wandering way of life is slowly disappearing.

The Quashgai (KASH-guy), the largest tribe, have been traveling for generations with their flocks of sheep and goats. They move from their winter tent camps in the valley to their summer camps high in the southwestern Zagros Mountains. In the past, they owed allegiance to no government and followed their own tribal laws. For a number of reasons, including drought and limits put on their movement by the government, they have begun to settle down and become farmers. The sight of the Quashgai herders in migration, with their black goat-hair tents spread like dots across the vast and dramatic countryside, is still one of the most wonderful scenes in the landscape of Iran.

SAY IT IN FARSI

Here is how you would say some common words and phrases in Farsi.

Hello.	*Salom.* (sa-LOHM)
How are you?	*Hale Shoma Chetoreh?* (HAH-lay SHOW-mah chet-oh-RAY)
Thank you.	*Mamnoonam.* (mom-noon-AHM)
You are welcome.	*Khakesh me Konam.* (KAH-kesh may koh-NAHM)
Goodbye; may Allah take care of you.	*Khoda hafez.* (koh-DAH hah-FEZ)

Farsi words that have become part of the English language include *bazaar*, *saffron*, *turquoise*, *orange*, *lemon*, *peach*, and *sherbet*.

The nomads of Iran live mostly on their own resources. Their animals provide them with meat, milk, and hides for their tents. The women spin and weave cloth for their clothes. Wool from their sheep makes the finest Persian carpets. They sell wool to get the money they need to buy the things that they cannot make or grow for themselves, such as salt, sugar, and cooking oil.

Dress in Iran

In the cities, most Iranian men dress in Western-style clothing, such as suits, slacks, jeans, and long-sleeved shirts. Most Iranian women today dress in traditional Islamic ways; their loose, dark-colored clothing often covers them from head to toe. At home, however, many women wear jeans and other Western-style clothes. Mullahs wear full-length brown or black robes and turbans—head coverings made by wrapping a long strip of cloth around the head.

Perhaps the most striking style of dress in Iran can be seen among the Kurds. Kurdish men wear baggy pants, an embroidered shirt, vest, turban, and sandals (or often, these

TRADITIONAL ISLAMIC DRESS

A chador is a piece of black cloth six to eight yards long, cut so that a woman can drape it over her whole body. With the addition of a *hejab*, or head-scarf, to cover her hair, a woman becomes a shapeless black figure when she goes out in public. In Shah Muhammad Reza Pahlavi's time, the chador was hardly ever seen. The Ayatollah Khomeini, however, instructed women to wear it in public for the sake of modesty and to follow strict Muslim standards of behavior.

Kurdish women wear brightly colored clothes in many layers.

days, sneakers). A wide sash with a dagger stuck in it and an embroidered skullcap under the turban complete the outfit.

Kurdish women wear many layers of clothing. A pleated slip is worn over red satin pants. Several *fistans*—long cotton dresses with zippers down the front—are fastened at the neck with big safety pins. The pins and zippers are meant to protect the wearer from the *khilbileeks* (kill-bih-LEEKS), evil spirits that come out at sundown, take the form of real people, and attack unwary humans.

Iranian families try to spend as much time together as possible.

3
FAMILY LIFE, FESTIVALS, AND FOOD

Rich and Ancient Traditions

Iranians are a very sociable people. They love to have visitors to their homes and to make them feel comfortable there. And in Iran, one's family is at the very center of social life.

Families eat together as often as possible. In fact, in the city, it is a custom for working fathers to go home for a two-hour lunch break. This arrangement causes two extra traffic jams a day in big cities, but it helps families stay close.

Often many generations of families live in the same house. For example, a child's parents, grandparents, and an aunt or uncle may share the home. This is called an extended family. Other members of the family often live nearby. By staying close, people in Iranian families take care of one another, from childhood to old age.

The Role of Religion

Religion is another important part of daily life. Nearly everything people do in Iran is related in some way to Islam. When Iranian Muslims greet each other, for example, they say something like, "I welcome you in the name of Allah." The Prophet Muhammad's name is used constantly in daily conversation. It is always followed by the words "Peace be upon him." In offices, workers are allowed a "prayer break," so that they can perform one of the five daily prayers that are required of Muslims.

Islam is a patriarchal religion. This means that Allah is thought of as male, and men are considered the "bosses," or leaders, of the family. In agreement with Islamic belief, men rule in business and in government, and they are considered the head of the family.

All Muslims are expected to face toward their holy city of Mecca while praying.

Many Iranian women are well educated. Some are doctors, lawyers, teachers, and even government officials. But, as Muslims, the women are always expected to obey their fathers, husbands, or brothers in important family matters.

Worshiping as a Family

On Friday, the Muslim day of worship, the mosque is an especially busy place. Iranian families gather there for the weekly prayer service. Before entering, they remove their shoes and wash their hands, faces, and feet in a fountain of running water. Inside, the mosque is cool. There

THE FIVE PILLARS OF ISLAM

Islam requires Muslims to follow these five "pillars" of faith:

1. Confession of faith: "I say that there is no God but Allah, and Muhammad is the Messenger [Prophet] of God"
2. Prayer five times daily
3. Fasting (going without food and water) from sunrise to sunset each day during the month of Ramadan
4. Alms-giving (charitable donations to the community)
5. Pilgrimage to Mecca, the birthplace of the Prophet Muhammad, at least once in a person's life

are beautiful carpets on the floors. Tiles painted with flowers and graceful writings from the Koran (cor-AHN)—the Muslim holy book—decorate the walls and dome.

Fathers and older sons stand shoulder to shoulder in long lines in the middle of the mosque. As they stand, they face a sort of pulpit. Mothers and daughters are behind them in a section reserved for women, separated from the men's area by a low wall. When girls are nine years old and boys are thirteen or fourteen, they may take part in the Friday services.

Celebration

Iranians love parties and other celebrations. Although it is frowned on by the mullahs, young people enjoy getting together in the evenings. With the window shades pulled down, they may watch music videos or dance to rock music. Relatives and friends of all ages often visit one another's homes. Families often go on picnics or gather together at home to enjoy a game of backgammon or chess.

National Holidays

Both city and country people enjoy festivals. There are two kinds of festivals in Iran. The first are national holidays. They celebrate such events as the overthrow of Shah Muhammad Reza Pahlavi and the founding of the Islamic Republic. Sometimes, hundreds of thousands of people march in parades on these holidays.

National holidays are also a time for visiting the cemetery. The most popular cemetery in Tehran is Behesht-e-Zahra, south of town. Here are most of the graves of the young men, some of them as young as ten or eleven years of age, who were killed in the war with Iraq during the 1980s. Families come in a steady stream to place fresh flowers on the graves of their sons and brothers.

Some holidays in Iran include a military parade as part of the celebration.

Behesht-e-Zahra is also a special place for Iranians because the Ayatollah Khomeini is buried there. When he died in June 1989, he was buried, according to his wishes, in a plain, unmarked grave. Later, people covered the grave with a green-roofed screen enclosure. It is now topped with an enormous golden dome that is visible from miles away.

Religious Festivals

Iran's most important festivals are religious. Ramadan, a month in which Muslims do not eat each day between sunrise and sunset, ends with the holiday of Eid el-Fitr (eed el-FIT-ter), the "Breaking of the Fast." When the new moon rises on the last day of Ramadan, a mullah announces the end of the fast, and a cannon booms. Families sit down to a great feast. They eat lamb, and there are special snacks, sweets, and huge bowls of rice. Those who can afford it or who have food left over share with the poor. No one goes hungry.

Iranians also celebrate the birthday of the Prophet Muhammad. This celebration is called Mouloud (moo-LOOD). On this day—which varies from year to year based on the Islamic lunar calendar—the whole family goes to the mosque (or, in small villages, to the *Husseiniyeh*, "House of Hussein," which serves as the house of worship). At bedtime, parents tell their children stories about Muhammad and his family. This reminds youngsters that the Prophet's family should be the model for all Muslim families.

Ashura is a day to remember the murder of the Prophet's grandson Hussein, in A.D. 680. Sunni Muslims do not observe it, but for the Shias of Iran, Ashura is a day of mourning. There are parades throughout the country—on city streets and dusty village roads. People cry aloud and beat

On Ashura, a troupe of actors displays their colorful costumes.

their heads and chests in sorrow. Special plays called *Taziyeh* (tah-ZEE-ya), or "Mourning for Hussein," are put on by groups of actors who go from village to village, town to town.

No-Ruz

The most important festival in Iran—and the happiest—is No-Ruz, which means "New Day." It is the beginning of the Iranian New Year. The origins of No-Ruz go back long before Islam.

No-Ruz always begins on March 21, the first day of spring. There is much to do in an Iranian household before that date. Around March 6, seeds of wheat or lentils are planted in a shallow dish and put in a window to grow. Houses are given a thorough cleaning. Carpets are taken outside and cleaned. Those who can afford it buy new clothes for the whole family, even if it is only one garment each.

The week before No-Ruz, a candle is set in each room and kept burning. This symbolizes the sacred fire of the Zoroastrians. On the morning of March 21, a table is set with the Koran, bread, a mirror, and a candle. The table must be set with seven symbolic items. As many of the items as possible should be green, for this color brings good luck. An egg is placed on the mirror, along with a leaf in a bowl of water. When the egg rolls across the mirror and the leaf moves across the water, No-Ruz has begun.

No-Ruz is a time for visiting with relatives and friends. Parents or older family members usually stay at home in the first days of the New Year. It is a time for giving children money and other presents. There are special sweets and drinks, and people are encouraged to eat all day long!

The thirteenth day of No-Ruz is considered unlucky. On that day, to chase away bad luck, families throw out the dish of green shoots that has been growing. Then they go out to the country or to a park for a picnic. These two activities are supposed to bring good times and good luck to the family.

Live sprouts (right) *are part of the special table setting for the festival of No-Ruz.*

"Food, Glorious Food"

The famous explorer Marco Polo supposedly said "Food, glorious food" when he first tasted a Persian melon, on his way from Italy to China. The same could be said about all Iranian dishes. Iranians enjoy a great variety of delicious foods. The only thing that most Iranians do not eat is pork. According to the Koran, the pig is "unclean."

The basis for much of Iranian cooking is *chelo*—cooked rice. Rice is grown mostly along the coast of the Caspian Sea. It is long-grained, light, and fluffy. Iranians may mix *chelo* with vegetables or even fruit. *Chelo* and meat together make Iran's national dish, *chelo kebab*.

Iranians in many towns visit local markets where they buy fresh fruit and vegetables.

NAN-E SHIRINI COOKIES

5 egg whites   1 tablespoon grated orange rind
1 cup sugar   1 cup chopped walnuts
2 tablespoons lemon juice

1. Preheat oven to 350°F.
2. Beat egg whites in a large mixing bowl until frothy. Add the sugar slowly, mixing until the egg whites are stiff.
3. Mix in the orange rind and lemon juice. Then blend in the chopped nuts.
4. Drop spoonfuls of the batter onto a greased cookie sheet. Bake for 30 minutes or until golden brown.

Makes about 20 cookies.

An Iranian dinner table will also have side dishes, called *sabzi khordan* (SOB-see-COR-dan), or "edible herbs." We might call them appetizers. These dishes include fresh parsley, chives, dill, tarragon, mint, and red radishes, with feta cheese and walnuts. The radish is probably the most popular vegetable in Iran.

Bread is a staple of the Iranian diet. In the villages, homemakers bake their own bread. In the cities, bread is bought from the neighborhood bakery. (Every city neighborhood has its own bakery, candy and ice cream shop, grocery, and shoemaker.)

There are four common varieties of bread. *Barbary* is crisp and salty, with a latticed crust. *Naan*—the general name for bread—is flat and pancake-shaped. *Lahvosh* is a very thin, brittle bread, while *sang-gak* is thick and chewy.

One of the family usually goes to the bakery in the morning to buy the day's bread hot from the oven. If any bread is left over after the day's sales, the baker will sell it cheaply to "bicycle breadmen." These people go from door to door on their bicycles selling the leftover but still fresh bread.

41

People in Iran enjoy a wide variety of sports—including hang gliding.

4

SCHOOL AND RECREATION

Busy Lives, Happy Lives

In the 1940s, perhaps only 10 percent of the people in Iran could read and write. Even in the 1960s, only 30 percent of Iran's population could do so. The only schools were one-room huts where boys—no girls were allowed—would sit and memorize the Koran, verse by verse. The students were supervised by a strict teacher who was armed with a cane. Whenever a boy made a mistake, the cane would come down across his knuckles. A boy who could recite the Koran from memory was considered educated.

A very small group of families who could afford the fees sent their brightest sons to religious schools called *madrasehs* (MAH-drah-sahs). There, after many years of study, they might become scholars like the Ayatollah Khomeini. As for girls, their education came from helping their mothers at home or tending sheep.

In the 1960s, Shah Muhammad Reza Pahlavi decided to set up a Western-style educational system in Iran, with primary schools, high schools, colleges, and universities. The

Iranian girls now go to school, but they must cover their hair.

subjects studied in these schools would be similar to those studied in the United States. The shah's main concern was to give all Iranian children a basic education. This meant teaching them to read and write.

The shah also formed the Literacy Corps. (*Literacy* means being able to read and write.) Instead of doing their military service, young high school graduates would teach reading and writing in villages where there were no schools. In some areas, these villages were so remote that they could be reached only by helicopter.

The Literacy Corps was very successful. Many village children—and their parents—learned to read and write. In addition, many of the volunteer teachers helped improve village life. They built roads and schools, planted trees and vegetable gardens, dug wells, and repaired *qanats* in their spare time.

Other schools were set up to teach soldiers—most of whom came from villages and had never been to school—how to read and write. Factory workers were given a pay raise if they could learn to read and write and pass a test on the machines they used in their jobs.

These programs brought about a great increase in literacy in Iran. Today, about two thirds of the population can read and write.

Time for Fun

Iranians are very fond of sports, but they are not familiar with body-contact sports such as football, except through television. However, they love to play soccer. Nearly every village

Soccer is the favorite sport of many young boys in Iran.

has its own soccer field, where boys meet after school to play. The game of soccer is not from Iran originally. It was introduced in Iran by Christian missionaries about 150 years ago.

The favorite game in Iran is chess. Iranians say that they invented the game. It was played in the Persian Empire more than 2,000 years ago. In the time of Shah Muhammad Reza Pahlavi, one would often see two elderly men sitting on a bench in a park with a chessboard between them. Today it is

THE RASHIDS GO TO SCHOOL

It is early Saturday morning, and the Rashid children are getting ready for school. The father, Hassan, has already left in his little car to fight Tehran traffic on his way downtown to the bank where he works. The mother, Sara, is getting breakfast for the children. This meal consists of *naan* bread, feta cheese (made from goat milk), honey, and tea.

The children eat quickly. Muhammad, the older child, is in fifth grade and must be at his school by 7:30. Malika, his sister, is in fourth grade. Her school starts earlier because she must be in line in the courtyard for prayers by 7:15. Muhammad puts on a hospital-type blue jumpsuit over his jeans and sneakers. Malika is already dressed in her school uniform of a blue wool skirt and blouse, with a child-size chador over it. Their mother throws a chador over her housedress and walks them to the doors of their separate schools.

The school week in Iran starts on Saturday and lasts until Thursday noon. There is a light lunch of fresh fruit, dates, pistachio nuts, bread, and cheese. Malika and Muhammad study reading, writing, and arithmetic, plus the history of Iran, social studies, geography, civics, and general science.

After they finish elementary school, they may take an entrance exam to get into high school. If they pass, they will begin learning English. This is now the second language in Iran because of its importance in the modern world of business, computers, satellite communications, and science.

Skiing is one of the many sports enjoyed by Iranians.

played mostly at home, with fathers teaching their sons the moves and rules of the game.

Another game that some believe the Iranians invented is polo. It was originally called horse-ball. The game was played by teams of riders, four to a side, trying to hit a small ball into a net with metal-tipped sticks, or mallets. Polo was called the "sport of kings" because only rulers and wealthy noblemen could afford to raise and train the fine horses used in polo matches. Even today, it is a rich man's game. Polo requires great skill on the part of riders because the ball must be hit

47

A young boy puts the finishing touches on an ornate gold bucket in a crafts shop.

5
THE ARTS

A Quest for Beauty

Iranians have made important contributions to art and literature. Persian miniatures—small paintings on glass, paper, or animal skin—are known around the world for their beauty. The mosques and palaces of certain Iranian cities, such as Isfahan, are among the most beautiful examples of architecture in the world. The art of landscape gardening was probably first developed in ancient Persia. And Persian carpets are not only useful, but they are also works of art in themselves.

Art in Small Packages

Islam in general—and the Koran in particular—does not allow artists to show the human form or face in artwork. But the Iranians' love of nature and of living things made them refuse to obey this ban. The result was the development of miniature painting.

In most miniatures, there is a phrase along one border praising Allah. But most of the paintings show scenes of people doing things—going on picnics, hunting, drinking tea—or shahs receiving visitors at court. The miniatures were made small so that the figures could not be mistaken for real people. In that way, the artists could not be charged with breaking the laws of Islam.

The great days of the miniature painters were in the time of the Turkish rulers, in the 1500s. Shah Abbas I was a supporter of painters and invited many to his court at Isfahan.

The art of miniature painting is still very popular in Iran. Iranian books of children's folktales often have fine miniature illustrations that bring the stories to life.

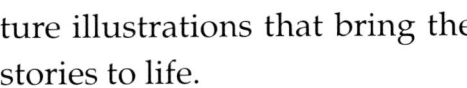

This old mosque in Isfahan has a striking dome. Two minarets are shown at right.

The Art of Building

In the ancient Persian Empire, buildings were usually gigantic in scale. Many of them had paintings and sculptures on the walls. These works of art showed kings receiving visitors, accepting the surrender of defeated enemies, and doing other things that proved their power. The ruins of Persepolis show how enormous these buildings must have been.

When the Iranians were converted to Islam, the emphasis in architecture changed from palaces to religious buildings. The mosque became a special feature of the Iranian landscape.

The first mosques were simple in shape, with a square central area, a roof of palm fronds supported by poles, and rush mats on the ground. As time went on, they became permanent structures, with domes and towers. Each mosque had a central dome and one or more towers called minarets. *Minaret* is a Farsi word meaning "lighthouse." The towers got this name because they could be seen from very far away in the desert. Each minaret had a walkway around it. The muezzin (moo-eh-ZEEN), who called people to prayer, would stand with his megaphone, or loudspeaker, below the minaret's pointed top.

Lovers of Gardens

Perhaps because the desert is all around them, the people of Iran especially appreciate green gardens with flowers, trees, and the sound of water. The Koran describes Paradise—Islam's heaven—as a garden filled with flowers and trees heavy with fruit. There, the wind rustles in the leaves and water splashes in fountains.

Long before the arrival of Islam, the emperor Cyrus laid out the world's first landscaped garden at Persepolis. It had a central pavilion called a gazebo, surrounded by flower-beds. Brick walkways led to pools of water. Tall cypress trees and sycamores were planted to provide comfort and shade from the hot desert wind.

Iranians are very fond of roses and may have been the first ones to grow them in gardens. They were also the first to grow pomegranates—a small tree with orange-size fruits full of sweet-tasting seeds. Many Persian miniatures show garden scenes with pomegranate, peach, and pear trees; date palms; and grape arbors.

The Persian Carpet

Iranian carpet weavers are some of the most highly skilled workers in the world. In fact, they are more than simply workers—they are talented craftspeople. The result of their effort is not only a product—it is a work of art.

There are many different designs in Persian carpets, depending on where they are made and by what group of people. Kurdish carpets often have animal figures. In the center of carpets from Baluchistan may be the tree of life—a symbol that goes back to the days before Islam. Whatever the design, no two Persian carpets are exactly alike.

Fine new carpets are sometimes put outside so that they will look more aged and can be sold as "antiques."

Visitors to Iran are often surprised to see beautiful carpets lying in city streets. There are two reasons for placing carpets on the street. The first is that driving over them has the same effect as hanging them up and beating the dust out of them, but it is less work. The second reason is that driving over a new carpet makes it look old, thereby increasing its value. Prices for antique carpets may go as high as $200,000 each! Sales of Persian rugs bring millions of dollars a year to Iran.

WEAVE A PERSIAN CARPET

Imagine yourself as a child weaver, a girl of ten, in a tent of the Quashgai people. You are sitting in front of a loom. What do you do? It is your first carpet. You have watched your mother weave on the loom, and you know that you have quick fingers and good eyes. Now you say the prayer she has taught you: "In the name of Allah, the Kind, the Merciful." This helps you to get started.

You take a length of dyed wool yarn and pull one end of it through the warp (the lengthwise threads of the loom). Thread the yarn under and around the right-hand warp thread, up between it and the next warp, and under and around the left-hand warp thread. After you have made knots at each end, weave two thin weft (horizontal) threads over and under the warp threads all the way across the loom. Press them down with a comb tightly to the row beneath. With a sharp knife, cut off the knot ends at the length of the pile (thickness) of the carpet you are working on.

Girls are often taught at a young age how to weave the distinctive Persian carpets.

If you follow this method for the next three years, repeating the knots 7.2 million times, you will have made a nine-foot-by-twelve-foot carpet. Weavers who have power looms can weave up to three carpets a year. Carpet manufacturers whose rugs are made on machines produce them faster than the best home weaver, but the quality is usually not as good.

Other things besides tying knots go into making a fine Persian carpet. The choice of dyes is very important. The best dyes come from natural sources such as rose petals, pistachio and walnut shells, and vine leaves. Each dye color has a meaning. Red means happiness or wealth. Turquoise keeps away the evil eye. Orange means faith in Allah. White is the color of grief or death and consequently is not used much except in some border designs. Green is also rarely used because it was considered a sacred color associated with the Prophet Muhammad. When weavers make a green carpet or put in a lot of green, they mean for it to be hung on a wall and not walked on.

Poets and Poetry

Poetry has always held the place of honor in the literature of Iran. The country's poets are highly respected. Many poets were given salaries to live at the courts of the shahs and write verses praising their ruler.

There are many poets writing in Iran today, but the most popular ones lived hundreds of years ago. Firdausi, the author of a famous work called the *Shahnama*, wrote entirely in verse. His tales of legendary kings and heroes take up thousands of lines of poetry. Even so, Iranians memorize and recite long passages from the *Shahnama*. Copies of the book are often illustrated with miniature paintings.

The most popular poet in the country is Hafez. He lived in the A.D. 1300s in Shiraz, often called the "city of poets" because so many of them lived there. Hafez wrote nearly 700 poems. They are filled with clever sayings and observations about human behavior. Iranians believe that when they are faced with a difficult decision, if they open a book of Hafez's poems, the first line that they read will tell them what to do.

The Iranian poet best known outside the country was named Omar Khayyam (high-YAM). He lived from A.D. 1048 to 1131. During his lifetime, Khayyam became famous as a mathematician and astronomer, a person who studies the stars and planets. People came from many other Islamic lands to study with him at his observatory in the desert near Isfahan. (An observatory is a building with a telescope, used for studying the heavens.)

Despite his scientific achievements, Omar Khayyam is most famous today for his collection of poems, called the *Rubaiyat of Omar Khayyam*. He is supposed to have written poetry just for friends, in his spare time. His poems might have been forgotten had it not been for Edward Fitzgerald, an English writer. In the 1800s, Fitzgerald, who knew Farsi, discovered Khayyam's poems in a dusty volume in a library. He decided to translate them into English. Omar Khayyam wrote his poems in four-line verses. In Iran, this form of poetry is called Rubaiyat. There are 250 Rubaiyat by Khayyam.

Music—Food of Love

Like poetry, music was always part of life at the courts of the shahs. Strolling musicians entertained at evening banquets. Poems from admirers to their loves would often be set to music. This music might seem strange to Western ears because Iranian musicians use a different musical scale.

Iranian musical instruments are also different from those in the West. The sitar, for example, is a broad-necked instrument with three strings. It is the ancestor of the guitar. The oud (ood), with its pear-shaped body and its hinged fingerboard, has six to thirteen pairs of strings, which are plucked. It is an early form of the lute. These instruments make pleasing sounds that soothe and calm every listener. It is pretty music from a people for whom so much of life is a quest for beauty.

Musicians play haunting Iranian melodies on their ancient stringed instruments.

Country Facts

Official Name: Jomhuri-ye Eslami-ye-Iran (Islamic Republic of Iran)

Capital: Tehran

Location: in the Middle East, bordering Iraq and Turkey (west), Armenia and Azerbaijan (northwest), Turkmenistan (north), and Afghanistan and Pakistan (east). The Gulf of Oman and the Persian Gulf lie to the south; the Caspian Sea is to the north.

Area: 636,294 square miles (1,648,000 square kilometers)

Elevation: *Highest:* Mount Damavand, 18,386 feet (5,605 meters). *Lowest:* Caspian Sea coast, sea level

Climate: desert or semidesert with little rainfall, except along Caspian Sea coast, which is semi-subtropical

Population: 64,625,455. *Distribution:* 57 percent urban, 43 percent rural

Form of Government: republic, but with supreme authority held by highest-ranking religious leader under laws of Islam

Important Products: *Agriculture:* rice, wheat, sugar beets, barley, cotton, tobacco, pistachio nuts, tea, melons. *Industries:* textiles, petrochemicals, food processing, oil refining, cement. *Minerals:* crude oil (petroleum), natural gas, sulfur, bauxite (aluminum ore), iron ore, coal, phosphate rock

Basic Unit of Money: rial; 1 rial = 100 dinars

Languages: Farsi (Persian), English, French, Arabic, Azeri Turkish, Kurdish

Religion: Islam (Shia sect), 95 percent of population; Islam (Sunni sect), 3 percent; others are Bahaism, Zoroastrianism, Judaism, Christianity

Flag: three horizontal stripes—green, white, and red—bordered with words *Allah o Akbar* ("God is Great") in Farsi writing; in center of white band is symbol of the republic, a drawing in red of the name *Allah* (God)

National Anthem: *Sorud Av Irani* ("Long Live Iran's Islamic Revolution")

Major Holidays: No-Ruz (New Year), March 21, at beginning of spring under Iranian 12-month calendar; Revolution Day, April 1; Ashura, 10th day of the month of Muharram in the Islamic lunar calendar; Eid el-Fitr, at end of the fasting month of Ramadan (varies yearly); Mouloud (birthday of the Prophet Muhammad) (varies yearly)

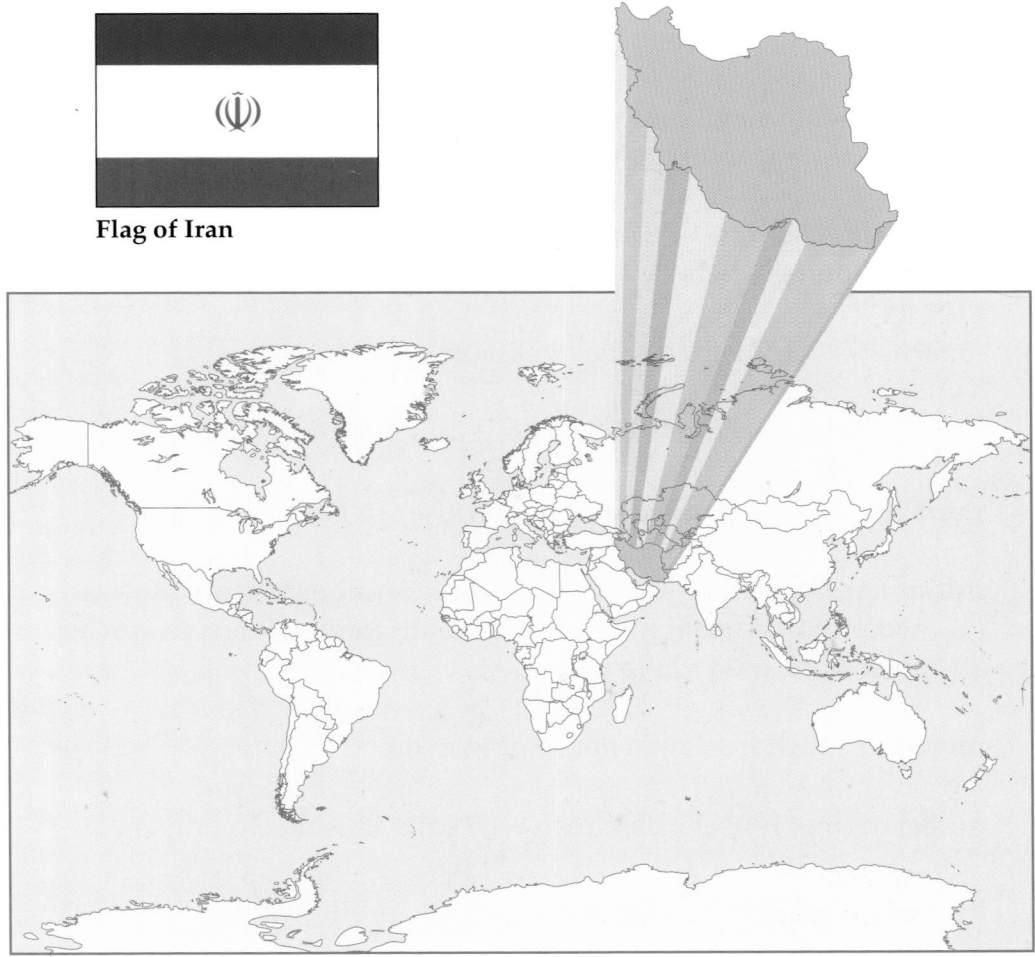

Flag of Iran

Iran in the World

Glossary

ayatollah (AH-yah-toh-lah): title given to pious and learned religious men; the highest-ranking **mullah**

chador (CHAH-door): body covering worn in public by a Muslim woman

dynasty: line of rulers from the same family who hold power for several generations

Farsi: main language of Iran, formerly called Persian

fistans (FEE-stanz): long cotton dresses worn by Kurdish women

Islam (ISS-lam): religion whose followers believe that there is one God, Allah, and that Muhammad is his prophet, or messenger

khilbileeks (kill-bih-LEEKS): evil spirits that come out at sundown, traditionally believed in by the Kurdish people

madrasehs (MAH-drah-sahs): religious schools

Majlis (MAJ-lee): Iran's House of Representatives

minaret: tower of a **mosque**; "lighthouse" in Farsi

missionaries: people—often priests, ministers, or others connected with a formal religion—who travel to foreign lands to spread their faith and to help others

mosque (mahsk): Islamic house of worship

muezzin (mooh-eh-ZEEN): man who calls Muslims to prayer

mullah (MOO-lah): religious leader of Islam; a Muslim teacher or scholar

Muslim: a follower of the religion of **Islam**

oud (ood): instrument with pear-shaped fingerboard and six to thirteen pairs of strings; an early form of the lute

qanat (KAH-nat): underground water tunnel used for irrigation

Rubaiyat: poem with four-line verses written with a specific rhyme pattern

shah: king of Iran

sheikh (SHAKE): tribal chief

Shia (SHE-uh): most popular branch of Islam in Iran; also called Shiite (SHE-ite)

sitar: broad-necked instrument with three strings

Sunni (SOON-nee): branch of Islam; outside Iran, most Muslims belong to the Sunni sect

turban: head covering made by wrapping a long strip of cloth around the head several times

Western: term referring to people and customs from Europe and North America

Zoroastrians (sore-oh-AS-tree-uhnz): members of a religion that was once the official religion of ancient Persia

zur khaneh (zoor hah-NEH): "house of strength"; a combination gym and wrestling arena

For Further Reading

Fox, Mary Virginia. *Iran*. Chicago: Childrens Press, 1991.

Gordon, Matthew S. *Islam*. New York: Facts On File, 1991.

Husain, A. *Revolution in Iran*. Vero Beach, Florida: Rourke Corporation, 1988.

Lawson, Don. *America Held Hostage: From the Teheran Embassy Takeover to the Iran-Contra Affair*. New York: Franklin Watts, 1991

Lerner Publications, Department of Geography Staff. *Iran in Pictures*. Minneapolis, Minnesota: Lerner Publications, 1989.

MacMillan, Dianne M. *Ramadan and Id al-Fitr*. Hillside, New Jersey: Enslow, 1994.

Rajendra, Vijeya, and Gisela Kaplan. *Iran*. Tarrytown, New York: Marshall Cavendish, 1992.

Sanders, Renfield. *Iran*. New York: Chelsea House, 1990.

Stein, Conrad. *Iran Hostage Crisis*. Chicago: Childrens Press, 1994.

Index

Page numbers for illustrations are in boldface

About the Author

Dr. William Spencer has taught the history and politics of the Middle East for many years. He has lectured at Florida State University, Rollins College, and other institutions of higher learning. He is the author of numerous books for adults on the Middle East.

Dr. Spencer grew up in Erie, Pennsylvania, and has degrees from Princeton University, Duke University, and the American University in Washington, D.C. He has served with the United Nations agency UNESCO in Paris, France, and in Morocco.

Dr. Spencer lives in Gainesville, Florida, with his wife, Elizabeth, an artist.

BOSTON PUBLIC LIBRARY

3 9999 03057 617 5

CODMAN SQUARE

WITHDRAWN
No longer the property of the
Boston Public Library.
Sale of this material benefits the Library.